CW00537094

how to romanticize your life

Joyful Tips and Advice to Elevate Every Day

Sophie Golding

An Hachette UK Company
www.hachette.co.uk

Vie Books, an imprint of Summersdale Publishers
Part of Octopus Publishing Group Limited
Carmelite House
50 Victoria Embankment
LONDON
EC4Y 0DZ
UK
www.summersdale.com

Printed and bound in Poland

ISBN: 978-1-83799-466-3

This FSC® label means that materials used for the product have been responsibly sourced

Substantial discounts on bulk quantities of Summersdale books are available to corporations, professional associations and other organizations. For details contact general enquiries: telephone: +44 (0) 1243 771107 or email: enquiries@summersdale.com.

Introduction

What's the first thing that pops into your mind when you hear the word "romance"? Is it sunsets? Flowers? Candlelit dinners? Sure, those are romantic, but romance is not all grand gestures and being swept off your feet; sometimes the little things can make the biggest difference. This book will teach you how to inject meaning and feeling into the everyday things we do for ourselves and for others. When you romanticize your life, and make the ordinary extraordinary, you will find beauty in what seems to be even the most boring chore. Make every moment magical, and an opportunity for joy.

Laying the foundations

Building a more romantic life for yourself starts by taking your own thoughts into consideration: nothing is more romantic than actually being heard. Before you do anything else, take a moment to think about what you need rather than always putting others first. Wear comfy clothes if that's what makes you feel good, eat healthy food to give your body what it needs, and understand the difference between the urgent and the important, replacing "I don't have time" with "Why don't I take the time?" Make yourself your first priority.

Then, try to be someone you'd like to spend time with: smile more, be more positive, more patient with yourself, find your sense of humour and fun. Whatever it is that you enjoy, you are the one who decides who you are and what things will make you feel good. Own your successes and your failures, and admire yourself for all of them: once you love yourself, you won't feel so dependent on the love of others!

Once you've got this far, you can start adding other touches to your daily routine that will bring a sense of romance and joy – every day is your day!

THE MORE YOU
PRAISE AND
CELEBRATE YOUR
LIFE, THE MORE
THERE IS IN LIFE
TO CELEBRATE.

Oprah Winfrey

Romancing yourself

Making your everyday routine a little less, well, "everyday", will help you fall back in love with life again, with the added bonus of massively contributing towards your overall well-being. Take care of yourself the way you would like to be taken care of by others, considering everything, from running yourself a candlelit bath to making yourself a special meal, getting out into the fresh air and treating yourself to the occasional lie-in. Be kind, always. The most important relationship you'll ever have is the one you have with yourself.

START EACH DAY WITH A POSITIVE THOUGHT AND A GRATEFUL HEART.

ROY T. BENNETT

Say yes!

What could be more romantic than saying yes? You could even argue that it's the most romantic word in the dictionary. This week, say yes to every positive opportunity that comes your way, and see where it leads you. Say yes to pleasure and joy, to the unexpected, and to experiences that you wouldn't usually be open to, even if it feels scary! If the answer to the question "Will this make me happy?" is yes, then definitely, always, wholeheartedly accept and enjoy the adventure.

Watch with glittering eyes the whole world around you, because the greatest secrets are always hidden in the most unlikely places.

ROALD DAHL

Set the mood

You don't need to go out and about to feel the love; you don't even need to be in anyone else's company. Simply making a romantic atmosphere at home for yourself can make ordinary moments feel special. It might only be Wednesday night, and you might have nothing in particular to celebrate, but take the time to create a cosy mood anyway: set the lighting, put on your favourite music, get into your cosiest PJs and give yourself a hug. In just a few minutes, you'll have made your day just that little bit more magical.

Know yourself

Just as you wouldn't necessarily fall in love with someone you've never met before, you need to know yourself in order to love yourself. Write a list of things that make you feel strong, that bring you happiness or make you fall crazy in love. Using a journal to commit what you are grateful for to paper (including positive things about yourself) will help you elevate your day. What did you do today that was truly lovely?

The universe is full
of magical things
patiently waiting
for our wits to
grow sharper.

EDEN PHILLPOTTS

Notes to yourself

Sometimes it's the tiniest little gesture that can make you feel the warmest inside. Not "box of jewellery" tiny, more the kind of small, beautiful things that come absolutely free: write yourself some positive notes to stick up around the house, or fold them into a jar to pick out at random when you need a boost. Use encouraging words that acknowledge what a great person you are, and bask in them when you read them later.

Be kind to future you

The daily mental load can suck the life out of even the most upbeat of us. How lovely would it be for someone to tick even just one of the items off the daily list? Be that someone, and do something nice for your future self, for example, prepare your breakfast the night before. When you wake up, it will feel as if someone else has lightened your load, sending you out into your day with a gentle kiss on the forehead. You can thank yourself tomorrow.

I choose to
make the rest
of my life
the best of
my life.

LOUISE HAY

Infuse with love

Over half of the human body is made up of water, so it's essential that we remain hydrated in order to stay healthy and keep our skin looking radiant. It doesn't have to be a chore though! Add slices of lemon or cucumber to your daily jug, or even quarters of a peach with mint leaves. If you prefer sparkling water, serve in a flute and savour the bubbles as you would a fancy champagne. There's no reason not to transform the simple act of drinking water into something more exciting!

Whistle while you work

Chores are inevitable, but you could make them magical with the right tune. Doctors at the Karolinska Institute of Sweden found that humming for at least 20 seconds each day can make you up to 15 times happier than not! Humming releases a generous dose of dopamine, melatonin and endorphins into your body, which will make chores feel a lot less mundane and a lot more joyful. Why not have a little dance while you work, or imagine yourself in a movie montage or music video? Next time you're dusting around the house, don't forget to use your new superpower to transform this boring task into a session of music and fun!

The element of surprise

The most romantic gestures often come in the form of an unexpected surprise, and even though it sounds counterintuitive, you can add some of that surprise to your everyday life yourself. For example, try painting the inside of your wardrobe a bright, flashy colour, or tape a picture that makes you smile to the inside of a cupboard, so that every time you open the doors you feel the small thrill of the unexpected. Repetition and routine have many strong positives, but the magic of seeing something out of the ordinary will inject some much-needed fantasy into your daily system.

Even TV night can be special

Don't spend yet another evening scrolling through social media while a reality show drones on in the background. Make your TV binge more mindful and romantic by setting the mood on the sofa first: create cinema vibes with some popcorn to eat while you watch, throw a super soft blanket over your legs, make a fort using the sofa's cushions, use the theme of the movie you've chosen to decorate or dress up before you sit down... However you choose to do it, make your next TV night an extra special event!

Every single day, do
something that makes
your heart sing.

Marcia Wieder

Dance party

Studies from Harvard Medical School have shown that dancing not only helps reduce stress, but it also increases levels of the feel-good hormone serotonin. Feeling stressed about doing chores around the house? Curate an upbeat playlist to move your body to while cleaning. Once you've finished, keep the party going and celebrate your accomplishment with a full-blown boogie around your living room. Soon you'll be looking for excuses to clean so that you can get those party vibes all the time!

Go green

Studies have shown that placing plants in a room can improve your mood and create an increased sense of well-being. This is because nature inspires positive, hopeful emotions, and to feel lighter and happier, the human body benefits from being surrounded by the colours that are all around us on this beautiful planet. So, add some foliage to your living areas; you could even use artificial ones if you're not that keen on watering your plant babies. Even artwork depicting leaves and flowers hanging on your walls, or flowery curtains that frame your windows, can help you feel the plant love.

When in doubt, take a bath.

MAE WEST

Soak it up

With just a few small changes, you can easily transform your bathroom into a beautiful, relaxing spa experience. The first, obvious steps are to light some candles, put on some gentle tunes and add relaxing bubbles to your bath water. You can go further by swapping the more traditional choice of bubble bath for deliciously scented salts, essential oils or even some natural food dye to add colour. For an extra special bath time, why not go full Cleopatra and add rose petals and some powdered milk to the water – it can do wonders for your skin! You'll soon feel like royalty.

Crack out the good plates

Why are you waiting for someone special to come over before you get out your best dinnerware? You deserve the special stuff, too! Even when it's no one's birthday, and even if you haven't got anything in particular to celebrate, plan a candlelit dinner with your fanciest crockery: it will make that midweek meal feel like a real event. You could even go the extra mile and choose a theme to stick to when cooking, decorating the table according to the meal. It's date night, for date night's sake.

Apply the same rule to your good tea set as well: put away the boring old teabags and that mug you got as a promotional gift. Brew yourself a real pot of tea for once, with tea leaves, served in your best teacup and saucer. Now pretend you're at the palace, entertaining royal guests. That porcelain isn't much use to anyone locked away in the cupboard.

These small tweaks only take a few extra minutes, but you'll have elevated something formulaic into a tiny celebration. Life's short, so treat yourself to a beautiful ritual whenever you can.

Think outside the box

Romanticizing your life takes creativity, but being creative isn't just about knowing how to use a paintbrush or crochet a bright, patterned blanket. It's about thinking outside the box, stripping away the usual limits and exploring the unknown areas hidden in the shadows of routine. Get off the bus at a different stop to discover a new place. Decide that today you will only eat things that start with the letter B. Or why not take an ordinary object and think of three different ways to use it? Is that an old DVD, or could it also be a necklace, a plate or something to spread butter with?

CREATIVITY IS
THE ABILITY
TO LOOK AT
THE ORDINARY
AND SEE THE
EXTRAORDINARY.

Dewitt Jones

Colour me happy

A beautiful sunset, a vivid rainbow, a cloudless sky... bright colours lift us up and have a positive influence on our mood. Take some time to appreciate the wonderful technicolour world you live in every day. Close your eyes and imagine the world around you in black and white. Now open them again, and count how many colours are actually there. It's amazing that what seemed ordinary just a moment ago is now bursting with life! Next, use your newly attuned colour senses to choose your outfit, and make sure you wear the colours that make you happiest. If your wardrobe is full of black and grey, why not add a colourful accessory to your jacket, or paint your nails a bright shade of red or orange? Doing that next load of laundry might seem more fun if you get a tiny flash of happiness every time you see your hands. You can also create an immediate colour boost to your surroundings by adding a bunch of flowers to a room in your house; don't wait for someone else to give them to you – go get your own!

The magic of
a good book

If you're longing to fall in love, find a good friend, go on a great adventure or just get that warm, fuzzy feeling inside, there's nothing like immersing yourself in a good book. But being totally relaxed while you read is an important part of enjoying the story: turn reading into an event by carving out a cosy "book nook" somewhere in your home. All it takes is a comfy chair, a blanket and some soft lighting to be whisked away from the very first page.

There are
many little ways

to enlarge
your world.

Love of books is

the best of all.

JACQUELINE KENNEDY ONASSIS

Sort it out

Enchant your living space by
implementing some simple changes
that don't include throwing everything
away. If what gives you joy is the
chaos of random objects, try at least
organizing them by colour, texture,
shape or size. Group all of your books
by colour to create a rainbow library or
collate all of your photos and postcards
onto one single wall. Introducing
symmetry into your life will make you
feel more serene. If you feel like a bigger
change, rearrange all of the furniture
in a room to see the space with a
completely fresh set of eyes. It's magic!

Enjoy brief moments

There is something very freeing about making something without worrying about the result, or about what its use will be – just creating something for the pure thrill of the process. Blow some bubbles, draw a flower in your coffee foam, make a mandala in the sand. Enjoy your creation, even if it only lasts for just a moment. Whatever you do, don't be tempted to take a photo before it goes!

Animals are the best

There are now hundreds of scientific studies that have shown that interacting with animals is immensely beneficial for humans. A few minutes spent stroking a cat can dramatically decrease levels of the stress-inducing hormone cortisol, and walking a dog is a fantastic way to tackle feelings of loneliness while getting some good old-fashioned fresh air and exercise into the bargain. Take a moment to really appreciate the time spent with animals, whether that's with your own pet, a friend's, or a dog you bump into in the park. Remember you're not only taking care of them – you're doing wonders for yourself, too.

What greater
gift than the
love of a cat?

CHARLES DICKENS

Second chances

Taking the bins out: not so romantic, right? Wrong! A bag full of rubbish could in fact be crammed with possibilities! Clean out that unusual glass bottle and make it into a vase. Repurpose that old tin of baked beans and make it into a lantern. Once you get into the swing of it, you might never get rid of anything again! And every time you see your new creation, you'll feel great that you saved it from being thrown away forever.

Listen out loud

There is a music to the world that we sometimes forget to hear when we get too caught up in our daily business. Whenever you have a moment, close your eyes and try to really hear the world around you: listen to the birds outside your window, lift a shell (or a cup) to your ear and imagine the sea in the air's whispers. Even better, try reading something out loud, and enjoy all of the different sounds that you are creating with the words. Listen to the silences between the words, too. Feel how wondrous the music of the world really is and your day will become a little more magical.

Music washes away from the soul the dust of everyday life.

BERTHOLD AUERBACH

YOU: AN ORIGINAL SOUNDTRACK

The best movie you'll ever see has to be the one that you're actually living right now, and music is sure to play a huge part in that. Try making a soundtrack of the ten most important songs that punctuate your past: choose a tune that reminds you of a specific time or place, close your eyes and listen carefully. Take a trip down memory lane, then decide if the track deserves its place on the ultimate list. Once you have your ten, you can enjoy the movie of your life anytime you want!

Let's get physical

Because we live in a world that puts so much emphasis on what we see, we often don't realize how much information we're receiving through physical touch. Next time you're doing the dishes, notice how it feels when the water is running through your fingers. Or try experimenting with different materials in your wardrobe: does a silk scarf make you feel extra special? Does a soft jumper make you want to snuggle up on the sofa? If brushed cotton feels luxurious, maybe it's time to get some new sheets and allow your whole body in on the experience!

Touch has a memory.

JOHN KEATS

The scent of nostalgia

Have you ever smelled something that made a memory flash before your eyes? Our sense of smell is very tightly linked to our emotions, and the receptors in our noses can remember up to 50,000 different odours! Find the smell that links you to your favourite memory – perhaps it's the sweet aroma of baking, or the hopeful scent of freshly cut grass – and try to recreate it at home by making your own cake, mowing the lawn (if you have one) or lighting a scented candle. Let the smell infuse into your environment for the day, as if you had managed to travel back in time, and live in that memory for a while. Or even better, make new habits to revisit the feeling whenever you like!

Eat with your eyes

Every meal begins with your eyes, so don't miss out on making the routine act of cooking more sensual: arrange the food artfully on the plate, perhaps organizing the ingredients by colour, or stacking the elements as if you were in a fancy restaurant. Browse the internet to get some inspiration, and before you know it, you'll become your very own Michelin star chef.

FAMILY IS NOT AN IMPORTANT THING. IT'S EVERYTHING.

Michael J. Fox

Who do you think you are?

Connecting with your family can create a sense of belonging and heartwarming nostalgia. Ask relatives what they know about your family history whenever you have a chance, but in the meantime, feel closer to them every day by following family rituals: cook the recipe that was handed down to you through the generations, and don't wait for a special occasion to use whatever heirlooms you have picked up, such as fancy table linen or your grandmother's brooch.

START THE DAY RIGHT

Romanticizing your life begins with one person – you – and making yourself feel special can start from the minute you wake up. Reward yourself by starting each morning with a self-care routine that will set the tone for the rest of the day: even before you set your first foot on the ground, allow some time to take in what's happening around you. Don't reach mindlessly for your phone, first tune in to the different sounds outside. What can you hear? Birds? Sirens? Silence? As soon as you stand up, root your feet into the floor, put both of your hands on your heart and say, "I love myself." No one can love you better than you can.

On your way to prepare your morning beverage, congratulate yourself – maybe you didn't want to get out of bed this morning, but you did! You were brave! Then, really savour the flavours and sensations with each sip. Taking the time to appreciate every detail in your morning will help you focus on elevating the other moments in your day.

Bonus points if you get up early enough to catch the sunrise!

BE YOURSELF; EVERYONE ELSE IS ALREADY TAKEN.

OSCAR WILDE

Personalize something

Some of the tools we use on a daily basis are so mundane that we don't even notice them any more. But why not personalize them to become more exciting and unique? Take that notebook you use every day at work: why not jazz it up a bit with some stickers, or go full glam and cover it in glitter? The same applies to the door you go through mindlessly every time you leave the house: try painting it a fun colour, or simply attaching a seasonal wreath to transform it into something that makes you smile every time you come home.

Spice it up

Make your own spice blends to transform each time you cook into a travel adventure: if you fancy a passage to India, try blending ground coriander, cumin, garam masala, turmeric and mustard seeds. Or if you're in the mood for wearing your sombrero, try some chilli powder, oregano, paprika and cumin. A trip to the souk? Grab your cinnamon, ginger, cumin and cloves. Or maybe it's the Caribbean you're longing for: so reach for the cayenne, paprika, basil and thyme. Every time you set foot in the kitchen, you could be going on a faraway journey, and you won't even need a passport.

Nighty night

A great bedtime routine elevates a daily obligation, putting a beautiful full stop to the day and giving you a chance to reflect on everything that has happened. Create a ritual each night to accompany your last moments before sleep: pamper yourself with an indulgent skin-care routine, then make a relaxing hot drink and write down the things that made you feel grateful during the day. Spritz your pillow with some sleeping potion (which you can buy or make yourself, using witch hazel, water and essential oils) and congratulate yourself for another amazing day on this planet.

Enjoy every minute

Forget about how crammed the train is, or how jammed the motorway is sure to be. All of that dreary stuff can be overcome by injecting some "you" time into them. Use your commute to rise above everything and elevate your mind with audiobooks and podcasts. Filling the dullest part of the day with joy will mean that you'll soon be looking forward to the journey instead of dreading it. You could also create a car karaoke playlist for an entertaining drive; the acoustics will be amazing!

You can find
poetry in your
everyday life,
your memory,
in what people
say on the bus,
in the news, or
just what's in
your heart.

CAROL ANN DUFFY

Baked messages

Biscuits, cakes and other baked goods are already amazing as they are, obviously, but you can make them even more interesting by decorating them with love! Take inspiration from the sweets of your childhood and use colourful icing to write delicious messages to your loved ones – or even to yourself! You'll get a special boost with every bite.

Keep the little things

Only keeping "important" items as we declutter our homes might seem a little intense; no one likes throwing away their belongings. But try switching the process around. Allow yourself to attach importance to things that don't seem to have any use, and don't feel guilty for keeping useless items around if they make you happy, for example, an old birthday card or childhood toy. Place them somewhere visible and enjoy the pleasure they give you every time you see them.

Take a forest bath

Take a leaf from the Japanese art of *Shinrin-yoku*, or forest bathing, and enjoy the different moods that trees offer according to the seasons: the dappled light of spring through new leaves, the crunchy yellows and russets of autumn underfoot. Look for insects and birds, touch the moss and the bark. Trees are magical, majestic beings, rooted deep and connected to the Earth while always reaching up towards new heights; immovable in the face of the chaos that surrounds them. Be more like the trees.

Trees are poems
the earth writes
upon the sky.

Kahlil Gibran

Stop, look and see

Exposing your body to natural light has huge medical benefits, but while you're out stimulating your vitamin D production, why not try really committing to the appreciation of what's happening around you. We're often too caught up in our habits and to-do lists to really see the magic that surrounds us, but spending an hour at the weekend sitting in the park, or even just stopping for 5 minutes on the way home from work can open your senses to a parallel universe that you might have missed. Take a pen and notebook or journal with you and draw what you see, or write down how you feel about the things you notice that you would usually have ignored. Look up and find shapes in the clouds, bend down and focus on the busy lives of the insects underfoot. Try to see the beauty in all of the tiny details that are all around you.

Not in doing what you like but in liking what you do is the secret of happiness.

J. M. BARRIE

Aisle adventures

Shopping for groceries can quickly become a tedious chore. Have you noticed that, stuck in a shopping rut, we often shop in exactly the same order each week? Try shaking things up a bit next time you're at the market or in a shop: steer your trolley into an aisle that you never visit, stop to look at what you've been missing, even if you don't buy anything. Pick up an exotic ingredient that you have never used before, even if you have no idea what to do with it; who knows what adventures you'll unlock by trying it out!

Join a club

It's easy to get stuck in a dreary routine as our lives settle down, but participating in a shared activity can help break that monotony, not to mention boost self-confidence and reduce loneliness. Those dark, wet Tuesday nights won't feel so bleak if you're dancing them away to the sounds of salsa music or the beats of a Zumba class. Or maybe whacking a tennis ball as hard as you can will get your spirits up. Whatever sprinkles that magic dust for you, get involved in a club to feel great; you might even make some interesting human connections along the way...

Let there be light

Light is a vital ingredient to feeling joy. And while the best way to charge up those happy thoughts is to get outside and feel the sun on your face, don't neglect the light sources inside your home: get rid of that intense single ceiling bulb and set up different shades of lighting for your walls, your floors, specific furniture and flat surfaces. Hang up some fairy lights, add floor lamps to dark corners, or install dimmer switches to create different vibes for different occasions. You'll feel like you're in a luxury hotel suite in no time.

Try stargazing

Stargazing is a magical experience. Children find it easy, and even fascinating, to think about space. Try to reconnect with that feeling, to think about the infinitely big and infinitely small; about all of the mysteries of the universe. Now, consider this: you are a part of that universe! We are all connected to a magical, complex whole, which is much bigger than our individual selves.

Tonight, if the sky is clear enough, take some time to admire the stars: lie out in your garden, or a nearby park, and try to spot constellations. If you don't know any, you can use a stargazing app on your phone, which will overlay your position with a map of the night sky, but you could also just make up your own names instead; after all, that's what constellations are – shapes that our ancestors decided they could see in the sky!

Spending some time gazing in awe and wonder at the sky above will not only put things into perspective for you, it will also reconnect you with the idea that we are truly surrounded by beauty every single day.

TWO THINGS
YOU WILL NEVER
HAVE TO CHASE:
TRUE FRIENDS
AND TRUE LOVE.

Mandy Hale

Best friends forever

Think of your friends: they're not just individuals, completely separate from you. You're a little part of each other's worlds, and the branches of your stories wouldn't exist if you had never met. Your strong friendships really are some of your most amazing assets; they allow you to grow, reflect and become more than just the sum of your parts. Make a list of all the friends you've had, from your very first BFF to the most recent acquaintance you've made. What have they taught you? What trace have they left? See your friends for the truly wondrous beings they are.

Fika time

In Sweden, *fika* means "coffee break", but it also describes the act of taking a break in and of itself. It's a time to stop and chat about the weather, or something deeper, but more importantly to take part in a friendly, merry ritual that you can only feel in the actual presence of the person you are sharing the moment with. Organize to meet someone "in real life" for coffee, a picnic or even just a walk instead of chatting over the phone or by text. Nothing can replace actually being in the physical presence of each other.

Day at the museum

Visiting a museum is a soul-enriching experience in itself, and looking at art can provoke visceral, subconscious, even intimate reactions. But art has more significant, magical properties than just that: since 2018, Canadian doctors have been prescribing their patients a visit to an art gallery as a form of therapy. Being in the presence of something beautiful is enough to disconnect you from the tedium of everyday life and elevate your day, even if it's just for a few moments. Do something amazing for yourself: get close to a work of art as soon as possible.

Give something back

What might seem like a mundane thing to you could be an essential lifeline for others, and volunteer work can have the power not only to make a difference to the world, but it can elevate your own sense of self, too. Dust off your cape and become a real-life superhero by investing your time in helping a local charity, or even by getting into the habit of making small but meaningful gestures, such as donating online or leaving a bigger tip than you usually would.

Here's an idea: have you heard of the Italian concept of *sospeso*? By paying for two coffees when you buy one, the second can be given to someone who can't afford it, making your own taste that much sweeter. Ask your local coffee shop if they fancy starting the tradition or, next time you're standing in line to get coffee to go, discreetly tell the cashier that you're leaving some extra money to pay for the drink of the person behind you. You won't see their reaction when they find out that their coffee is free that day, but you will feel like a better person all day long. You'll have brightened their day, and your own.

Magic is a method of talking to the universe in words that it cannot ignore.

NEIL GAIMAN

Land art

Leaves, stones and twigs might seem small and insignificant, common as they are on your everyday path. But try building them into tall, balanced structures, or arranging them by colour to form a picture, and suddenly you've created something beautiful. Spice up your daily walk and make the ordinary world feel more extraordinary by creating stunning artwork using nothing other than Mother Nature's treasures.

If you have
the ability
to love, love
yourself first.

CHARLES BUKOWSKI

Dear me

There's nothing lovelier than receiving a personal letter. Don't wait for someone else to send it, though: write one to yourself! Tell yourself what you love about your life right now, how you feel and what makes you happy. Writing a letter to your future self will not only allow you to gain some perspective on what you are going through today but it may also help future you appreciate a time when you didn't necessarily have everything you strived for. Once you close the envelope, put it aside and plan to open it in exactly a year.

Try something new

It might feel safe to stay sheltered from the things you fear, and even pretend that they don't exist. But don't be afraid of failure! Failing just means that you actually tried in the first place! Do something new and far removed from your everyday routine to feel good about your fears. Start a new instrument or try a new recipe, and if that's too scary, just try wearing something really flashy. You might feel self-conscious, but you might also enjoy the new freedom of expression.

It is never too late

to be what you

might have been.

GEORGE ELIOT

Find your alignment

Walking – for many of us, it's the most ordinary thing in the world, right? Wrong! The act of putting one foot in front of the other is a small miracle when you consider what's in play. The following alignment technique will help you discover a newfound appreciation for this simple, everyday activity.

Stand with your eyes closed, and feel yourself anchor through your feet into the ground. Imagine a piece of string that runs from the top of your head all the way to space. Stand straight, in alignment with that string. Now walk ahead using this new posture and be grateful for how amazing it is that you can move your body forward in this way.

If walking isn't possible, you can find the same alignment from a sitting position. Make sure your pelvis is positioned correctly under your back and neck, and use the crown of your head to elongate your spine. Whatever position you are starting from, project strength and confidence as you move forward, and you'll start to feel better in no time.

Happiness is there for the taking – and making.

OPRAH WINFREY

Have a mini adventure

When a routine slowly sets into place, even what used to be a fun activity can become boring and repetitive. If you always walk to work the same way or use the same path when you're running, try spicing it up by turning each outing into a mini treasure hunt. Make a list of things to spot while you're out: a cat, someone wearing a hat, a red car, a smile... Make a map of your findings when you get back, and change the list to become more and more challenging each time – if you dare!

Pretty as a picture

We all have a running to-do list, either in the back of our mind or on paper, stuck somewhere like the fridge door. But writing words can sometimes feel flat and scholarly, and the list can become unwieldy, haunting you from wherever you keep it. Make your chores lighter by writing them down in a more entertaining way. For example, use sketch-noting, which conveys messages using only pictures – a drawing of a telephone to remind you to pay your mobile bill, a pretty flower as a prompt to water the plants... Pay attention to colours and pen types, and find yourself looking forward to writing down your next important task. It's more fun, and potentially easier to remember, depending on your style of memorization. You might even find yourself wanting to frame your beautiful, finished list forever!

For fast-acting relief, try slowing down.

LILY TOMLIN

Taking it slow

If we are travelling at the same speed as the things around us, or even faster than them, we can't appreciate how they are moving, or that they are moving at all. What wonders are we missing as we zoom down the motorways of our days? Try standing still at rush hour and watch how the flow of people parts and rejoins around you. In the quiet of the woods, stop and try to detect the insects flying past your ears. Even when you aren't moving, the world continues; enjoy that feeling of stillness in the midst of the busy world around you.

A smile is a
curve that sets
everything
straight.

PHYLLIS DILLER

Smile!

Remember that time when you first
fell in love? You had that smile on your
face for hours, so much that it hurt
your cheeks! Smiling is a fast, free and
sure-fire way to lift your mood, not
to mention make you look and feel
beautiful! Do it as often as you can.
Find a picture that makes you smile,
and hang it up somewhere you will see
it every day. Or find a cushion with
words on it that lift your mood when
you sit down. Every time you smile, your
face will shine and your day will improve.

The best day ever

Our schedules are so full of jobs and household chores that we sometimes forget to set time aside simply for the things we *want* to do, not *need* to do. Create a "bingo card" of activities that make you happy: watching a movie on a big screen, taking a walk in the woods, chilling out in your PJs... Don't set any limits, the only rule is that it's something that you don't *have* to do. See how many you can cross off in one day this weekend, and when you complete a row, give yourself a bonus treat!

BEAUTIFUL
DAYS DO NOT
COME TO YOU.
YOU MUST WALK
TOWARDS THEM.

Rumi

Embrace your inner child

Remember when you used to play dress-up? When make-believe was part of every single day? You can recreate that joyous feeling every time you apply your moisturizer or make-up, or even just take a shower and wash your hair: imagine that the soaps and creams in your bathroom are the magic potions that will transform you! Or, you could start making time to reconnect with your favourite childhood pastimes, such as baking cakes or playing frisbee in the park. Life is more fun when you embrace your inner child and get your imagination flowing.

Turn back time

Sometimes, a memory resurfaces that makes us nostalgic, but not necessarily sad. Embrace those beautiful memories. You can also use them to make your life more playful: are there any clothes in your wardrobe that remind you of your youth? Get out those bell-bottoms or that shell suit and pretend that you are your younger self for the day. Not because you wish you were younger, but because it's fun to remember how you were! You could even organize a fancy-dress party and get your friends in on the action. Don't forget to curate a good soundtrack to sing to!

Your own muse

When you look in the mirror, do you tend to focus on your best qualities, or the little imperfections that you'd like to change? Zoom in on your best assets by drawing a self-portrait: if you're good with a brush it could be in the form of a painting, but you could also try making a collage of what you like most about yourself, or writing down a list of your qualities that starts with each of the letters that make up your name. You deserve to be a muse, even if just your own.

The star of your own show

You might not believe it, but your life is every bit as worth writing about as a celebrity's. Start writing the first chapter of your autobiography and see what bubbles up to the surface. Not only will you have an opportunity to realize how fascinating your life has been until now, but you'll have something lovely to read again in a few years, too. Your life is a novel, you just don't know it yet.

What's the title of your movie?

Ever felt like you were currently starring in a movie that also happened to be your life? You should: every moment of every day has the potential to become the scene of a movie. It doesn't have to be extraordinary, either; even the dullest chores are interesting with the right lighting and background music. Put your phone or camera somewhere with a good view and just let life unfold. And if you aren't satisfied with the result, no problem: you can just rewrite the scene and film again!

If you don't fancy staging a whole movie, why not choose a single moment in your day to record; it could be a whole event, or simply just one single instant. If you commit to filming just a few seconds of your life every single day, at the end of the month or the year you can collate them to get a beautiful snapshot of everything that you felt counted. Time to look at your life through the lens of your own camera. And... action!

Put yourself first

We spend so much time doing things for others, and worrying about what other people might think or feel about our actions. When was the last time you did something just for yourself and no one else? Do something completely alone today: go to the cinema without telling anyone, treat yourself to an ice-cream sundae even if you don't have anyone to share it with, write something you've never told anyone on a piece of paper and then throw it away or burn it. Be your own best company.

Perfectly imperfect

A life less perfect is so much more interesting than something fresh out of the pages of a magazine. Embrace the beauty of the asymmetry of life by picking up a piece of pottery from a local artist: sure, that mug might not have the clean, round lines that would qualify it for the shelves of a big-brand shop, but that's its real beauty! The bumps and curves are proof of the love that was put into its creation. Each irregularity is a reminder of the human touch that made it. There is real perfection in imperfection.

IF YOU CAN DREAM IT, YOU CAN DO IT.

WALT DISNEY

Daydream

Sometimes creativity doesn't come to you, you need to go on a quest to find it, and nothing is better for that than a good old daydream. The Japanese language has a word that fits perfectly: *boketto*, or "gazing into the distance without thinking of anything specific". It's a great way to let unexpected thoughts bubble up to the surface. Find somewhere quiet to sit and get your *boketto* on, preferably with a huge, open view (the beach, a hill, the top floor of the building) and let the immensity of the world inspire you.

THE POWER OF THE SUN

Have you noticed that even the most ordinary-looking street can look beautiful if a ray of sunshine hits it in just the right way? How the sea shimmers like diamonds when the sun is at its brightest? We don't just enjoy that effect because it's pretty – getting enough sunlight plays a vital part in keeping your energy levels high and healthy. As soon as you see the sun peeking out from behind the clouds, run outside and drink it in. Close your eyes and imagine you are soaking it up like bathwater; really let its warmth take

over your whole body. If you can't get out,
try placing a mirror or two close to a window
so that as soon as those rays come out, they
are being immediately redirected into your
room. The sun is the original supercharger
for your energy batteries.

Instead of worrying about what you cannot control, shift your energy to what you can create.

ROY T. BENNETT

Rewrite the noise

We are constantly being bombarded with noise, but all of the sounds we bathe in each day could also become the magical background music to your day. Next time you get annoyed or distracted by what's going on around you, close your eyes and rewrite the story. Inject some romance into the everyday noises you hear. That plane overhead: where is it headed? In what country will it land? Where is that train going, and who is on board? That bird outside the window: what could it be singing about? How far has it travelled to serenade you? Hear the story, rather than the clamour.

Your best coffee table book

How many photos do you have stored in your phone or computer; beautiful moments that you never take the time to look at any more? This seems like a waste of some wonderful memories, not to mention a risk – you could lose them forever if something happens to your device. Take some time to sort through them all and create your own coffee-table book. It's much more likely you'll flip through a gorgeous book to relive that fantastic family holiday than if it's locked away on a hard drive. And just seeing it again, in full colour and on glossy paper, might make you feel as though you've returned.

Look up

Pay attention to your eye line: do you usually look at the ground, or straight ahead of you in a glassy gaze that isn't actually "seeing" anything? Whenever you can, look up and marvel at what you've been missing – there is endless sky, just above your head! Lie down in the grass and find the shapes in the clouds. If it's a grey day, try to imagine what's happening behind the wall of mist. You can use this to add magic to every single day of your life; it's all happening right there, all of the time – don't miss it!

Life is not just about breathing. It's also about being breathless.

Alfred Hitchcock

Take your breath away

Most of us have had the pleasure of having our breath taken away at least once: by a person, an experience, a landscape or even a song. It's not only something that happens in the movies. Try and recreate that time by imagining something you can do for yourself or for someone else to get both of your heartbeats racing. It could be anything, from signing up for a day of sports to going for a romantic walk through the empty streets on a warm summer's evening. Whatever creates the surprise that will mark the day as one to remember.

Breathe in waves

Romanticizing your life isn't just about finding joy in the things surrounding you; it can come from within, too. Even the simple, fundamental act of breathing can be made more deliberate and important. Think of each breath as a wave: find the magic that is right there within yourself by counting as the wave comes in with your breath and floods the shore, and counting again as the breath leaves your body, and the wave retreats and disappears. You are a magician, and all you had to do to realize it is breathe!

Happy accidents

Instead of panicking when things don't go
to plan, make room for the random things
that happen in your life. Missed the bus?
That's a great opportunity to turn something
negative into a joyful experience: enjoy the
unexpected walk and make a point of noticing
something you would have missed along
the way. Optimism and curiosity often lead
to great opportunities, and seeing the silver
linings to your cloud will keep you available
for something better down the line. Stay
positive and watch the magic unfold!

Ask the right questions

Making your life more enjoyable can be as simple as changing negative statements into positive questions; examining problems from every single angle. Take that exotic holiday you're lusting after: instead of saying, "I can't afford it," try "What can I do to afford this?" or "How can I bring that holiday feeling to me?" Make a really detailed list, with even the craziest of schemes to achieve your goal. Be as imaginative as you want to! The answers might surprise and delight you, and you'll have made a difficult issue way more fun to tackle.

WHEN
YOU WANT
SOMETHING, ALL
THE UNIVERSE
CONSPIRES IN
HELPING YOU
TO ACHIEVE IT.

Paulo Coelho

Curiouser
and curiouser

Also known as "wonder-rooms", sixteenth-century "cabinets of curiosities" were collections of mysterious objects that were marvelled at, acting like a little museum at home. Try making your own wonder-room from random objects you have curated: have you ever found a single playing card discarded in the gutter, provenance unknown? Put it in the cabinet, next to that odd flower and the badge that brings you luck for some unexplained reason. Step back and admire your collection, feeling how wonderful it is that objects can be transformed to become beautiful just by the way we look at them.

For me an object
is something
living.

JOAN MIRÓ

Let the seasons guide you

There are opportunities to appreciate the wonder of the world around you throughout the whole year: notice young shoots peeping out in spring, even if only through cracks in the pavement, and feel effortlessly hopeful. In summer, close your eyes to bask in the warmth of the sun, linger outside a little longer and feel like time has stopped. Come autumn, admire the changing colours in the trees or find a crunchy pile of leaves to kick around. And in winter, marvel at the intricate patterns the frost leaves on the plants in the early morning. There is beauty everywhere.

Waste time

In these days of such strong emphasis on high productivity, we are all cursed with making sure that we are super-efficient with our use of time. But what if that didn't mean running around like headless chickens, cramming as many activities as possible into every minute? See each instant as a precious gift, and reevaluate how long it should take to do something. Next time your phone pings, don't look at it immediately – finish what you are doing first. Whatever it is will still be there in a minute. Get to it in your own time, not someone else's.

The most important thing is to enjoy your life – to be happy – it's all that matters.

AUDREY HEPBURN

Beautiful stones

Some people believe in the magical power of stones and crystals, and for them, certain stones have more power than others. But even if, for you, a stone is just a stone, next time you're enjoying a pleasant walk, try to find one that pleases you and admire its pretty patterns and colours. If you're a believer in the power of stones and crystals, bestow it with a secret power of your choice. Does it give you patience? Is it a magnet for positive thoughts? Try decorating it with a lovely message and placing it somewhere to make you smile when you see it, or put it back outside somewhere, for someone else to find!

Rewrite
the story

Romance is also the act of transforming reality into a fiction that pleases our right brain. Become your own Hans Christian Andersen and open up the magical version of the story of your life. Start by enjoying some people-watching and rewriting the stories of the characters you can see. Who are those people on that bench in the park: are they long-lost lovers? Is this their first date? And that man, walking with such determination down the street, where is he going? Who is he off to meet? Now try it with your own life: how would you write it if it was a novel for others to read? If you like, reverse the letters in your name to create a new character, and see what that person might do: Laura may be too shy in real life, but who is Arual? Oscar wouldn't dare speak up to his boss, but what would Racso do? You're in control of the narrative of your character, just as you are in your real life.

LIFE ISN'T
ABOUT FINDING
YOURSELF.
LIFE IS ABOUT
CREATING
YOURSELF.

George Bernard Shaw

Conclusion

Life is a beautiful, wondrous thing, and thanks to you, it can be full of romance every single day. As this book has helped you discover, you are the main ingredient in making your ordinary life extraordinary, so use its advice to inject beauty into every single day, and be kind, to others and yourself. Take chances. See mistakes as opportunities. Be happy on purpose. All you need to do is show up, and make sure you never become jaded with this world that, if you take the time to see it, is full of love and magic.

Self-Care

**How to Live
Mindfully and Look
After Yourself**

Claire Chamberlain

Hardback

978-1-78685-775-0

Self-care is the essential action of looking after your mind, body and soul. Dip into this book whenever your energy is flagging and choose one of its many quick and easy self-care tips, from gaining strength with invigorating walks and delicious, healthy food to treating yourself to a slow evening of face masks and hot soaks. This soothing collection of self-care ideas and inspiring words contains the pick-me-up you need.

Self-Kindness

How to Grow Your Happiness with the Power of Self-Compassion

Claire Chamberlain

Hardback

978-1-80007-440-8

Transform your relationship with yourself. Learn to deepen your self-love and grow your happiness with this beautiful handbook, filled with practical tips and actionable advice. Whether you're at the beginning of your journey to self-acceptance, or you're a seasoned self-love advocate, this book is the ultimate guide to embracing self-kindness and living a life with more self-compassion.

Have you enjoyed this book? If so, find us on Facebook at Summersdale Publishers, on Twitter/X at @Summersdale and on Instagram and TikTok at @summersdalebooks and get in touch. We'd love to hear from you!

www.summersdale.com

IMAGE CREDITS